ard

Address Only

HALFPENNY

W.P. COLLIER

Walter Percy Collier (1875-1937) began his photography business in Bellingham about 1912. Over 25 years, he produced many hundreds of pictures of Bellingham and the surrounding area. He was a familiar sight as he rode his motorcycle along the quiet roads and tracks of the lovely Northumbrian countryside.

The Heritage Centre in Bellingham has a reconstruction of the shop of W.P. Collier and stages a permanent display of his pictures, together with some of the photographic equipment that he used and sold.

INTRODUCTION

Walter Percy Collier was born on Merseyside in 1875 and began his working life as a draper. He came to Newcastle and worked for Harry Ord Thompson, a noted industrial photographer, who married his sister.

W.P. Collier learned much from Harry Thompson. His work was of very high quality. He rarely put his name on his photographs, which can be identified from the titling. The production of real photographs with individual titling is a characteristic feature of the work of W.P. Collier.

After his wife died in 1910, Walter Collier left Newcastle for Bellingham. He probably started his photography business around 1912. Some of his earliest pictures can be dated to 1913. W.P. Collier later served as an aerial photographer with the Royal Flying Corps in the final years of the Great War.

The period 1900-1935 was the golden age of the postcard. Telephones were still uncommon and people used postcards for messages. They would also buy postcards to record visits, especially as the more remote places could be visited in motor cars and charabancs. People collected postcards and carefully preserved them in their postcard albums.

The Collier collection forms a definitive picture of Northumberland in the period between the two World Wars. Though many of the original plates have been lost, the quality of the original prints, each carefully hand printed, means that we still have a wonderful view of bygone Northumberland.

THE SHOP OF W.P. COLLIER

Edie Lyons worked for W.P. Collier in the 1920s: "Mr Collier did not come from Bellingham but from Liverpool. He had three children, Jack, Muriel and Edith. His wife died before he came to Bellingham. The children stayed with relatives. Edith eventually came to live with her father. Edith and I worked in his shop. We were always together.

The shop had his name over the door. We opened at 8 o'clock in the morning and closed at 8 o'clock at night. We sold sweets, writing paper, tobacco and cigarettes. The shop was not very big. It would be full with four or five people in it and so we did not have many postcards on display. We kept them in boxes underneath the counter. People came in and we would put the boxes on the counter and they would look through. The same cards would be in each box. The shelves were red and went right around the shop. They were kept for bottles of sweets. The window was full of sweets and chocolate. We needed the sweets to carry us over the winter. I got paid 8/- a week when I started, and, before I left, I got 10/- a week.

There was a narrow passage where we did the developing and printing. We used plates about 6" square. The plates were bigger than the postcards. We put the plate into the exposing machine. The lamp was underneath and it shone upwards. We put the paper into the frame and brought the press down. This kept the paper in place. When everything was ready, we pulled the slide across, left the paper exposed for a few seconds, and then pulled the slide back. We counted five or six seconds out aloud. Then we took the paper out and developed it. If it was not satisfactory, we would do another one and count a bit more, or a bit less. Then we would do a batch. If part of the plate was a bit lighter than the rest, we would shade it with a piece of glass.

In the back of the shop, we did the washing and drying. We had three big water tanks, all connected to each other. It was so cold in the winter. After we had developed and fixed the pictures in the darkroom, we took them into the back room and put them into the first tank and let them run for quite a while, half an hour or more, and then moved them into the second tank, and then to the third one. When we thought that all the hypo was off, we took them out. We had large pieces of glass. We put the pictures face downwards and rolled them with a roller. This put the glaze on them. We left them drying overnight and, when we came in the next morning, they were ready to take off. Then we squared them off with a piece of wood and a cutter.

We would print quite a few pictures in a day, a hundred, or so. There was no machinery to do the printing. We started with oil in the lamp, then paraffin and then electricity. We enjoyed the printing, though the chemicals made our fingers yellow. We would develop and print films. A film cost 1½d to develop. The prints were 1d each.

Mr Collier would take wedding photographs but that was not his main interest. What he liked most was to go off on his own and take pictures. He enjoyed every bit of Northumberland. He would go off nearly every day. His camera was a large one and he would strap it on his back, tripod and all, and ride off on his motorcycle. He would take one plate of a view and, if it was not to his satisfaction, he would go off again and take another. He was a fit man and would walk miles to get the picture he wanted.

He went all over Northumberland, to the shops and post offices, with his sample books. He did not need to advertise much because he was so well known. There was a novelty in postcards: they sold for 1½d or 2d. We sold cards in the shop but people in the outlying districts would order them. If he had a request for his cards, we would get them printed right away and then he would ride off to deliver them, all weathers, on his motorcycle. He would never let anyone down."

HARESHAW LINN BELLINGHAM. 164.

BELLINGHAM

In the long descent to Bellingham, we see the town attractively spread out along the hillside, near to the cleft of the Hareshaw Burn.

A delightful excursion on foot is to Hareshaw Linn, a mile up the burn of that name from Bellingham.

One is soon following a winding course in a shady ravine that would be worth visiting without the final reward of the splendid force beneath a hundred-foot precipice.

Robert Hugill (1930)

On the Road to Bellinham Mart.

163 ROAD TO BELLINGHAM MART

A rustic view of Catholic Corner before re-alignment of the road removed the sharp bend to the left. The Roman Catholic church of St Oswald, built in 1839, lies hidden behind the trees and high wall in the top left of the picture. The picture captures the once common sight of a shepherd driving his sheep to market. These Cheviots are possibly from Newton, near Charlton.

BELLINGHAM

187

187 BELLINGHAM, TYNE VIEW

A nostalgic picture, reminding us of quieter days. Tyne View is on the right, Reed's School (now Reed's Hall) is on the left. The driver leads in the hay pikes on his bogie. He is probably Thomas Breckons. The little girl is not camera shy but some one else is hiding behind the bogie. Everyone looks towards the camera and keeps still, except for the horse, who moves just as the picture is being taken.

3

147 BELLINGHAM, FRONT STREET

Five children pose patiently in the middle of Front Street while W.P. Collier takes his picture around 1916. William Dodd was a tailor and draper. Edward and Frank Coulson were distinguished saddlers and harness makers. Mary Jane Hindmarch was a china and general dealer. The shop on the far right belonged to Miss E.M. Smith, newsagent and stationer, until she moved to Parkside.

145 BELLINGHAM, BLACK BULL HOTEL

Two men stand outside the saddlers shop and watch W.P. Collier taking this picture one overcast morning around 1914. Outside the Black Bull Hotel, one of four public houses at this time, stand beer barrels and a cart: the horse still reigned supreme. Displaying a large advertisement for M. Alexander, decorator and painter, the Town Hall on the left looks quite grand.

141 BELLINGHAM, ROSE AND CROWN INN

The Rose and Crown was a popular destination for charabanc parties of the 1920s. John Philipson was the landlord. His wife Lizzie would bake all sorts of things for the parties. After looking round the shops, or strolling up Hareshaw Burn, they would come back to the Rose and Crown for their teas, retiring to the back room. Walter James Turnbull made boots and shoes.

117 BELLINGHAM, FRONT STREET

A view of Front Street taken in the early 1920s. Horse and motor transport are equally represented. On the left is the drapery shop of Miss Smith and Miss Foster. It claimed to be the Harrods of Bellingham. On the right stands the shop of Mr A. Crester Wilson, a general dealer, who sold sweets and stationery. The shopkeepers of these times took pride in staging lavish window displays.

BELLINGHAM.   125.

125 BELLINGHAM, RAILWAY HOTEL

A 1920s view across King Street to the Railway Hotel, now the Coach House. It shows clearly the sloping platform, or coach dike, where passengers could board their carriages more easily. Thomas Hedley was a draper and tailor. W.P. Collier had his shop in Lock Up Lane, on the left. The notice board can still be seen. The shop behind the cyclist belonged to John Telford, who made clocks and watches.

143 BELLINGHAM, PARKSIDE

W.P. Collier seems to have taken his coat off for this picture, taken around 1914. Alec T. Low, Chemist and Druggist, has a fine window display of bottles and potions. Next door is Charlton's Commercial Temperance Hotel. Numerous small shops are evident along Parkside. The building on the right is the North Eastern Banking Company Ltd, which is now Barclays Bank.

BELLINGHAM 1584.

158 BELLINGHAM, BOER WAR MEMORIAL

The Union Jack flying from the Boer War Memorial may date this picture to 1919. The Sutherlands have left the Royal Temperance Hotel and Miss E.M. Smith, newsagent and stationer, has taken over the chemist's shop. The two boys are delivering milk for the Demesne Farm. The boy on the left is Willie Aynsley and the boy on the right is Stanley Smith, nephew of Mr W. Stanley Telfer, the butcher.

BELLINGHAM F.C. 1919-20.

BELLINGHAM FOOTBALL CLUB

Standing: Tom Hedley, Eddie Little, George Dagg (goalkeeper), Stan Telfer, Matt Sisterson, Bert Lamb. Sitting: Jimmy Little, Ridley Milburn, Tid Scott, unknown, Harry Pigg. The supporters include Teddy Dodd, on the left, with the cap, and, in the centre, the brothers Robert and Thomas Hedley, the tailor, both wearing large cloth caps. Billy Lawrence is smoking the cigarette.

142 BELLINGHAM GOLF CLUB c.1925

Sitting: Harry Walker, Matt Sisterson, Wilf Thompson, Jack Turnbull. Standing: unknown, unknown, Mr. Turnbull, Mr. Johnson, Mr. Johnson, William Warwick, William Aynsley. The original Club House, shown in this picture, stood by the Otterburn Road. In 1925, fees for visitors were 1/6d per day (Sundays from 1pm, 2/6d), 5/- per week, 7/6d per fortnight, and 10/- per month.

BELLINGHAM HOCKEY CLUB

Back row: unknown, Colin Nesbit, Violet Matthews, William Aynsley, Jack Thompson, Matt Sisterson, Tommy Milburn, Alf Hutchinson. Middle row: Teddy Johnson, Maisie Johnson, Helen Bell, Harry Glass, Jean Milburn, Roddy Thompson. Front row: George Milburn, Sarah Thompson, Jimmy Armstrong, Jean Bell, Bert Lamb. The picture was taken at Catholic Corner.

JUBILEE DAY. BELLINGHAM. MAY 1935. 3.

3 BELLINGHAM, JUBILEE DAY 1935

The Parade of the Children, escorted by their teachers, including Jean Milburn (in the round hat) and Frank Greener (in the smart suit). A Sports Day then followed in the grounds of Riverdale Hall, where the children received a Jubilee Day mug and a paper bag containing sandwiches and cakes for tea. This is one of several pictures which recorded the whole parade.

222 BELLINGHAM STATION

This 1930s picture, looking towards Reedsmouth, shows a neat Bellingham Station, on that part of the London & North Eastern Railway, which ran from Riccarton Junction to Hexham and Morpeth. Though never a commercial success, the line was important on market days and for schoolchildren. The line was formally closed on 15th October 1956, to the dismay of the local population.

1 BELLINGHAM MART

Fairs were once common. Hirings for servants were on the Saturdays before the 13th May and 11th November. The Wool Fair was on the first Saturday after July 20th. St Cuthbert's Fair was on the Saturday after September 15th. The fairs died as the marts for the auction of cattle and sheep, especially the autumn sale of sheep and lambs, became more important.

"BLOODYBUSH"
ON THE OLD DROVE ROAD FROM SCOTLAND.

NORTH TYNE

The Valley of the North Tyne is a peculiarly happy hunting-ground for the tourist. The road keeps long and close acquaintance with a stream whose endowments of sylvan banks, gently sinuous course, and placid waters are best summed up in the word gracious.

The North Tyne is an exception among Cheviot streams – it is wooded to within a few miles of its source.

Robert Hugill (1930)

TARSET.

1323

1323 TARSET BURN

In 1930, Robert Hugill described the route from Tarset to Falstone, via Donkleywood, as emphatically worthwhile for the cyclist, and for the motorist who does not object to a winding and rather neglected road. In this picture, the road descends steeply past Redmire Cottage to the elegant bridge across the Tarset Burn. This picture breathes the rural tranquillity that W.P. Collier enjoyed so much.

The Hott School and Post Office

153

153 HOTT SCHOOL

Opened in 1851 by the Presbyterians, the building could accommodate 50 pupils of all denominations. For the first 40 years, the teacher was Ralph Anstruther Macadie; in the 1920s it was George Britton Stanley, followed by Miss Margaret Dagg. For many years, Peter Robson ran Greystead Post Office and Grocery. The school closed in 1966 when a new school opened at Greenhaugh.

THORNEYBURN GARDEN FETE. 1927   (3)

3 THORNEYBURN GARDEN FETE

Wearing their best dresses, the girls pose round the maypole in the garden of Thorneyburn Rectory. The Rector is the Reverend George Hanson. The Church of St Aidan was built in 1818 by the Commissioners of Greenwich Hospital. Thorneyburn had a station but, as only two trains a week stopped there, on Tuesdays, most people used the station at Tarset.

FALSTONE STATION. 259.

259 FALSTONE STATION

The railway was the life blood of the North Tyne Valley, until its closure in 1956. Falstone station was typical of many on the North British Railway, single track for much of its length. It had a single platform, a loop line allowing trains to pass, sidings, offices, a station house and signal box. In the 1920s, the station master was Hector Inglis, followed by Archibold Brown Robertson.

152 FALSTONE, BLACK COCK INN

The sign over the front door of the Black Cock Inn reads W.R. Allcroft, dating this picture to around 1914. Next door is the Church of St Peter, built around 1815. Falstone also had a Presbyterian Chapel. Before the Chapel at Kielder was built in 1874, farmers from as far afield as Deadwater would walk with their dogs to Falstone. The dogs were left in the porch during the service.

SUMMER CAMP. WHICKHOPE. 1397

1397 WHICKHOPE CAMP

Situated on the Whickhope Burn, opposite Bull Crag, the Camp was built in 1930 to give work to unemployed men from Tyneside. Known as Dolies, they built the road from Whickhope to Cranecleugh, which was one of the first Forestry Commission roads. They put a weir into the Cranecleugh Burn. Kielder Water now covers all their work, except for a short stretch of road at Cranecleugh.

1560 PLASHETTS, GENERAL VIEW

On the left, the railway swings towards the station of Plashetts hamlet, with a few cottages, church hall and public house. On the right are the coal screens, a smithy, brickworks and rail incline which gave the only access to Plashetts Colliery, high above. The building with the smoking chimney is Plashetts Farm and the building in front is Hollinwood School House. All are now beneath Kielder Water.

"THE FARM" PLASHETTS. 1564.

1564 PLASHETTS FARM

The village lived for coal and died after its collieries were flooded during the General Strike of 1926. The Farm, which was uncomfortably close to the colliery workings, was the home of Mr John Thompson, his daughters Nell and Hannah, Miss Bell, the aunt who kept house, and Mr John Grieve, the shepherd who had lived there all his life. All are now beneath Kielder Water.

278 KIELDER STATION

Mr John Achincloss, the stationmaster, stands on the platform of the station, later renamed Kielder Forest. He ran a post office and coal agency for the isolated community and had several small warehouses. The coach house, built for the staff of Kielder Castle, was later used by local blacksmith, Mr Arthur Grimwood of Stannersburn, who would visit once a month to shoe horses.

PERCY CROSS OTTERBURN. 404.

REDESDALE

This is the finest main road radiating from
Newcastle, and most attractive in the vicinity
of the Cheviots, which it approaches by a
lonely valley and crosses by a picturesque pass
– the only true pass over the Cheviots, utilised
by a main road.

Otterburn, pleasantly situated near the Rede,
is interesting chiefly from its connection with
the Battle of Otterburn.

Robert Hugill (1930)

455 OTTERBURN BRIDGE

An early 1920s picture of the main road, looking west towards Jedburgh. The bridge across the Otter Burn was built in 1862. St John's Church can be seen to the left of centre through the trees. Two children pose happily for the camera, opposite the future filling station. The road surface is still rough, reflecting the era of the horse rather than the automobile.

402 OTTERBURN GARAGE

A late 1920s picture of the garage which Thomas Gibson opened around 1922. He sold petrol in two-gallon cans. The road surface is much improved. There is a fine display of petrol pumps to cater for the increasing motor traffic. There are numerous advertisements, including one for John Foster, an automobile engineer, who had open or closed cars for hire.

"MURRAY ARMS" OTTERBURN   396

396 MURRAY ARMS HOTEL

An early 1920s view of the Murray (now Percy) Arms, taken from the gardens that were to become the forecourt of Gibson's garage. Miss Isabella Snaith ran the inn for many years, as seen on the faded sign. Some fine automobiles stand outside, the one on the right apparently requiring some attention. The wall which curves round, on the right, enclosed the front gardens of private cottages.

451 OTTERBURN VILLAGE SHOP

Taken around 1922, this picture shows the Grocer and Draper shop, with its fine display in the window. It is now the Post Office. The lady on the left was Miss Margaret Mitchell, who ran the business until the late 1930s. The man was Thomas Robson who was brought up with the Mitchells and married the lady on the right who was Ann Marie Douglas.

POST OFFICE OTTERBURN

432 OTTERBURN POST OFFICE

This picture of Otterburn Post Office was taken around 1922 and shows Stanley Potts who was the sub-postmaster and owned the house. He left the position in 1933. The identity of the woman is unknown. The brass plaque denotes James Graham Miller, the local doctor. He was based in Bellingham but held a surgery in Otterburn on Tuesdays.

OTTERBURN HALL HOTEL. NORTH⁰.

OTTERBURN HALL HOTEL

A red brick Victorian mansion with stone facings, Otterburn Hall was the residence of Sir Charles and Lady Louisa Morrison-Bell, until their deaths in the 1920s. The Hall then became empty. Rebuilding followed a major fire in 1928, with the glasshouse section being finished by 1930. From that time, the Hall, with its extensive grounds, has offered accommodation for visitors.

Capt. Dawes Bi-Plane
Visit to Otterburn Hall
Oct. 25-27 1913.

1 CAPTAIN DAWES

Flying from York to Montrose in a Maurice Farman biplane, Captain G.W. Dawes of the Royal Flying Corps spent the weekend at Otterburn Hall with his aunt, Lady Louisa Morrison-Bell. The children of Elsdon and Otterburn schools were invited into the grounds to see an exhibition flight before the gallant captain continued on his way. One of the first datable pictures of W.P. Collier.

MILITARY HOSPITAL REDESDALE ARTILLERY CAMP.   11.

11 MILITARY HOSPITAL

In 1911, the War Office purchased the Featherwood Estate to use as an Artillery Training area. The first buildings to be erected were stables for the horses. The wooden hut, pictured above, served as a military hospital. In 1950, it became living quarters. It was demolished in 1970. The foundations are still visible to the North West of the modern camp.

"REDESDALE ARMS". HORSLEY. NORTH⁰.

419 REDESDALE ARMS HOTEL

Proudly displaying his new automobile stands Ben Prior who ran the Redesdale Arms from around 1926 until 1940. "What a character!" are the words used on one postcard to describe him. Still called the 'First and Last' by locals, and rebuilt after a major fire in the summer of 1993, the hotel remains an important point on the road between England and Scotland over Carter Bar.

453 ROCHESTER VILLAGE

Outside the taller building, members of the Leighton family watch a Vickers tank, reminding us of the All Arms Training Area. The building with the porch is Rochester Post Office. In the 1920s, Miss Mary Isabella Leighton was the sub-postmistress. Her brother, Norman Leighton, helped with the business and used his car to run children from the outlying districts to Rochester School.

CARTER BAR CHEYIOT HILLS

483

483 CARTER BAR

The AA and RAC signs proudly mark the achievement of reaching the English-Scottish border at Carter Bar, 418 metres above sea level. The telegraph poles will follow the main road all the way to Newcastle. W.P. Collier has skilfully used their silhouettes to emphasise the nature of the land which is always undulating and, in dull weather, often dreary.

Address Only

THE NEW BRIDGE
817 "LINBRIG" UPPER COQUET.

UPPER COQUETDALE

There is a road which goes to Barrowburn, but it is not as yet suitable for motoring. The cyclist can penetrate far into the hills and even pass by sheep-tracks over the watershed into Scotland.

Robert Hugill (1930)

A fellow called Collier used to come around and stay in Alwinton and take photos and family pictures. If I remember rightly, I think that he came from Bellingham.

Grace Hunter (née Dagg) (1935)

COQUETDALE MEET BY HOLYSTONE

785 COQUETDALE MEET

The Salmon Inn was kept by Mr & Mrs Emmerson for many years. The huntsman, with two of his companions, has stopped with his pack of fox hounds and border terrier to receive the traditional stirrup-cup. The fox hounds chase the fox, while the border terrier bolts the fox, if it goes to ground. The clothes that the landlady and the huntsman are wearing suggest a date around 1914.

825 HARBOTTLE VILLAGE

The village in the 1930s looking down the main street. The Gothic fountain on the left is the Clennell memorial, built in 1880. The Star Inn is further down. Every morning, Dr Henry Bedford attended the Dispensary on the right, where there is a glimpse of W.P. Collier's motorcycle NL 3770. This enabled him to take his camera to places, difficult of access even today.

"LINBRIG" + "LINSHEELES" UPPER COQUET. 773

773 LINBRIG & LINSHEELES

The old track up Coquetdale used many fords and footbridges: swing bridges served the two farms in this picture. By 1930, the ford which crossed the Coquet had been replaced by a new road which swept across the fields of Linbriggs Farm (on the right) to use the new road bridge. Linshiels Farm (on the left) got its road bridge in 1959. W.P. Collier's bicycle can be seen by the road.

776 SHILLMOOR

A fine 1920s view of this 2000 acre farm, standing at the foot of the Usway Burn and extending as far as Kidlandlee. The swing bridge was the only way of crossing the Coquet dryshod before a new road bridge was built to replace the ford, in the early 1930s. The bridge was built a little upstream of the ford, which can just be seen, opposite the two hay stacks.

786 BARROWBURN

This farm was central to the life of Upper Coquetdale, especially as the old road ran right across the farmyard. The new road runs nearer the Coquet, just behind the mounds of the tatie-pits. It was the home of such legends as Mary Barton, Eliza Murray and Mary Tait – three generations of ladies rooted in the history of Coquetdale. This was a favourite place of W.P. Collier.

858 BARROWBURN CLIPPINGS

Judging from the fleeces in the cart, clipping was already well advanced when this picture was taken at The Faads, near Barrowburn. The sheep folds are still in the same place. The girl who is busting (marking) the sheep is possibly Nelly Oliver, whose family shepherded Windyhaugh. She wears a large bonnet: a sun tan was the last thing a girl of the 1920s wanted.

826 USWAYFORD

Though well-supplied with paths and tracks, Uswayford was an isolated farm, even by Coquetdale standards, when this picture was taken around 1914. All provisions were left at Barrowburn, four miles away, and were brought up by horse and cart. A walled tatie-garth, two peat stacks and three hay stacks can be seen. These were essential to carry a family and the livestock through long winters.

ALWIN HILL MARKET PLACE. 839

839 ALWIN HILL MARKET PLACE

A charming picture, taken around 1914, at the foot of Kidland Hill. Access to farms was often difficult, so carriers would meet their customers at an agreed time and place. It was a chance to exchange news as well as buy and barter. The carrier in the foreground is Andrew Tully of Netherton. Other carriers were Robert Davidson of Harbottle and Matthew Read Wood of Alwinton.

CLIPPING SHEEP AT KIDLANDLEE   849

849 CLIPPING AT KIDLANDLEE

The clippers pose for the picture, taken about 1915. The boy on the far left is Alec Rutherford, the buster: he put tar on the newly clipped sheep either to identify them or to cover any nicks made by the clippers. The man holding the Kidlandlee mark (TK) is Henry Thompson. The skyline is dominated by the shooting box, built by Captain C.D. Leyland. It was demolished in 1957.

MUSEUM CHESTERS 18.

HADRIAN'S WALL

A small charge admits to the camp of Cilurnum, or Chesters, as it is more usually called, and to the beautifully-kept museum of Roman antiquities in a building behind the lodge-cottage.

The Roman Wall is additionally attractive by reason of the country it traverses — the middle portion is of as spectacular a nature as anything to be found in the north.

Robert Hugill (1930)

MUSEUM AND LODGE GATES

'CHESTERS'
HUMSHAUGH. 490

490 CHESTERS, MUSEUM

Chesters has always been a popular destination for visitors to the Roman Wall. John Clayton, a wealthy scholar, who owned six Roman forts, including Chesters, began the first of his excavations in 1843. In 1896, six years after his death, the Clayton Memorial Museum was opened to display the collection of objects found at Chesters and other sites on the Roman Wall.

BATH HOUSE
GENERAL VIEW

CHESTERS

59 CHESTERS, BATH-HOUSE

A view of the Roman bath-house, looking north, probably taken shortly before the Sixth Pilgrimage of the Roman Wall in 1930. The furnace was in the foreground and the entrance in the background. The absence of consolidation produces an evocative effect but the results of such neglect are plain to see and had "wrought sad havoc" as a contemporary scholar ruefully observed.

ROMAN WALL. HOUSESTEADS NORTH^D 32

32 HOUSESTEADS, KNAG BURN GATEWAY

Just east of Housesteads, this Roman gateway, discovered in 1856 and excavated in January 1936, allowed civilian traffic to pass through the Wall. The notice reads: *A charge of 6d each person will be made for admission to the camp. Tickets must be obtained at the Farm House and given up to the caretaker in the camp. Parties of over 20, 3d each. No dogs allowed.*

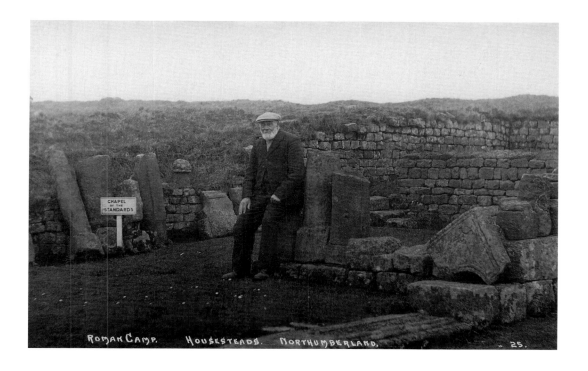

ROMAN CAMP. HOUSESTEADS. NORTHUMBERLAND. 25.

25 HOUSESTEADS, THOMAS THOMPSON

Thomas Thompson (1850-1938) followed his father as shepherd of Housesteads Farm and became caretaker of Housesteads Fort, first for the Clayton family and then for the National Trust. This impressive figure was familiar to thousands of visitors to Housesteads Fort. Born within the Roman ramparts of High Rochester, he had a broad Northumbrian accent and a deep interest in the Romans.

SOUTH GRANARY "BORCIVICUS" HOUSESTEADS. NORTH^D. 17

17 HOUSESTEADS, SOUTH GRANARY

In December 1931, the National Trust excavated part of the South Granary, easily identifiable from the sturdy foundations and rows of stone piers, which carried the joists of a wooden floor, which is no longer visible: this kept the corn dry. Judging by the camera and film pack on the table, W.P. Collier was not the only photographer interested in recording the results.

CRAG LOUGH. NORTHUMBERLAND.

2 ROMAN WALL, CRAG LOUGH

Taken from the top of the Roman Wall on Hotbank Crags, this outstanding view of Tynedale, looking west, was guaranteed to delight W.P. Collier. Hotbank Farm is on the left, partly hidden behind the plantation, while the Roman Wall, carried high above Crag Lough, sweeps away towards Steelrigg. At around 327 metres, Hotbank Crags are the second highest point of the Roman Wall.

CRAG LOUGH NORTHUMBERLAND.   12.

12 ROMAN WALL, CRAG LOUGH

Taken from High Shield Crags, looking east, this fine view emphasises the dramatic drop to Crag Lough, 20 metres below. The Roman Wall ran slightly to the south of the crags. All the land in this picture, including Crag Lough and Hotbank Farm, is now owned by the National Trust. The crags are popular with climbers while the lough provides private fishing: boats are moored on the east side.

41 ROMAN WALL, STEELRIGG

Named after the old farmstead, which has become the car park, Steelrigg remains a favourite starting point for a walk along the Wall. This view, looking east towards Hotbank Crags, captures the grim determination of the Roman Wall as it strides along the wave-crest of the great Whin Sill towards Crag Lough and Hotbank Farm. The worn grass bears evidence of the tramp of 1930s feet.

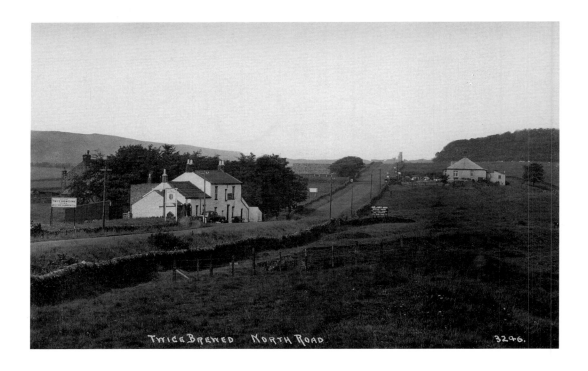

TWICE BREWED NORTH ROAD

3246.

3246 TWICE BREWED INN

The Twice Brewed Inn, *noted for the coolness of its cellars and the mellowness of its amber ale*, offered teas and light refreshments for walkers and day trippers. Further along, the Bognor Guest House, offered similar fare. Just off the picture, to the left, was the first Once Brewed Youth Hostel. Sir Charles Trevelyan opened this converted cottage with a tea party in October 1934. Its sign was a tea pot.

ROMAN MILE STONE   CHESTERHOLME   BARDON MILL.   27

27 CHESTERHOLM, ROMAN MILESTONE

A rustic view of the Roman Stanegate which linked Corbridge and Carlisle. This road, seen rising in the distance, originally ran in front of the milestone, seen in its original position on the right. The farm is Codley Gate, over which tower the walls of Roman Vindolanda. The ford across the Bradley Burn has been replaced by a shallow culvert, which is still prone to flooding.

59

"CHESTERHOLME" BARDON MILL 1819.

1819 CHESTERHOLM, VINDOLANDA MUSEUM

A nostalgic view of the cottage, built in 1831 by Anthony Hedley, a talented archaeologist, who conducted several excavations of Vindolanda between 1818 and 1834. Excavations were resumed in 1930 by Eric Birley and have continued to the present day. The cottage is now the museum of the Vindolanda Trust, which has made some outstanding discoveries about life on the Roman frontier.